FAITH'S LITTLE INST[...]
FOR FINA[...]

Supercharged Quotes To Build
God's Abundance in Your Life!

Harrison House, Inc.
Tulsa, Oklahoma

Faith's Little Instruction Book for Finances —
Supercharged Quotes To Build God's Abundance in Your Life!
ISBN 0-89274-837-0
Copyright © 1995 by Harrison House, Inc.
P. O. Box 35035
Tulsa, Oklahoma 74153

Introduction

Faith's Little Instruction Book for Finances is a unique collection of powerful, faith-building quotes from leading Spirit-filled men and women of past and present. These quotes, coupled with Scriptures, will strengthen and encourage you to stand firm and trust in the promises of God for your finances.

Based upon the original best-seller *Faith's Little Instruction Book*, this little book will challenge you to do more than stand by and watch things happen. It will move you into action to put God's Word into practice in the area of your finances. These quotes will stir your spirit as you read from Kenneth Hagin, Kenneth

Copeland, Gloria Copeland, Smith Wigglesworth, Paul Crouch, Kathryn Kuhlman, Joyce Meyer, Fred Price, Creflo Dollar, Jr., and many others.

This book is a treasury of wisdom from some of the greatest people of faith in our times, but more importantly, it is a treasury of the timeless wisdom and guidance of the Bible. *Faith's Little Instruction Book for Finances* was designed to be a burst of hope and inspiration — we pray that it is in your life!

The purpose for abundance is to preach the gospel, feed the poor and meet the needs of others.

Kenneth Copeland

He that by usury and unjust gain increaseth his substance, he shall gather it for him that will pity the poor.

Proverbs 28:8

5

It's the diligent man who ultimately prospers, who ends up in a position of power and leadership.

Bob Yandian

The soul of the sluggard desireth, and hath nothing: but the soul of the diligent shall be made fat.

Proverbs 13:4

The decision to live in poverty or to live in prosperity is yours!

John Avanzini

I call heaven and earth to record this day against you, that I have set before you life and death, blessing and cursing: therefore choose life, that both thou and thy seed may live.

Deuteronomy 30:19

Prosperity is not things, it is knowing God.

Ray McCauley

And this is life eternal, that they might know thee the only true God, and Jesus Christ, whom thou hast sent.

John 17:3

8

The biblical principles of success are built on faithfulness, trust, integrity, discipline and obedience.

Dick Mills

This book of the law shall not depart out of thy mouth; but thou shalt meditate therein day and night, that thou mayest observe to do according to all that is written therein: for then thou shalt make thy way prosperous, and then thou shalt have good success.
Joshua 1:8

The tithe is not a debt we owe, but a seed we sow.

Oral Roberts

In the morning sow thy seed, and in the evening withhold not thine hand: for thou knowest not whether shall prosper, either this or that, or whether they both shall be alike good.

Ecclesiastes 11:6

Everytime God gives you an opportunity to give, He is also giving you an opportunity to increase your income.

Mike Murdock

But this I say, He which soweth sparingly shall reap also sparingly; and he which soweth bountifully shall reap also bountifully.

2 Corinthians 9:6

11

Hard times are wrong times to stop giving to God.

John Avanzini

I have been young, and now am old; yet have I not seen the righteous forsaken, nor his seed begging bread.

Psalm 37:25

We plant by reaching out to others, then we reap as God reaches out to us.

T. L. Osborn

Give, and it shall be given unto you; good measure, pressed down, and shaken together, and running over, shall men give into your bosom. For with the same measure that ye mete withal it shall be measured to you again.

Luke 6:38

13

To be truly motivated
to success, we first
must know that it
is God's will for
us to prosper.

Charles Capps

So then faith cometh by hearing, and hearing by the word of God.

Romans 10:17

14

The world of plenty
all about you is
ample proof that
your heavenly Father
wants you to live
in abundance.

T. L. Osborn

*Then shall the earth
yield her increase;
and God, even our
own God, shall
bless us.*

Psalm 67:6

15

If you are serving a god limited in finances, then you are serving the wrong god.

Kathryn Kuhlman

The silver is mine, and the gold is mine, saith the LORD of hosts.

Haggai 2:8

16

Deliver us, Lord, from all the restrictions we put on your bountifulness.

Dick Mills

Thou preparest a table before me in the presence of mine enemies: thou anointest my head with oil; my cup runneth over.

Psalm 23:5

17

There is a way out of debt, and the Holy Spirit will give you tips on how to do it as you look to Him for help.

David Crank

For as many as are led by the Spirit of God, they are the sons of God.

Romans 8:14

18

If you have been obedient to give, then you should be expecting to receive a better job, a raise or new direction in business.

Charles Capps

19

You'll have no trouble tithing if you see God as your Source.

Marilyn Hickey

In the one case, the tenth is collected by men who die; but in the other case, by him who is declared to be living.

Hebrews 7:8 NIV

20

Make a habit of giving, whether your income is large or small.

Charles Capps

He that hath a bountiful eye shall be blessed; for he giveth of his bread to the poor.

Proverbs 22:9

21

Don't settle for "barely get along" or "just enough;" God's will is exceedingly abundantly above that.

Billy Joe Daugherty

And ye shall eat in plenty, and be satisfied, and praise the name of the LORD your God, that hath dealt wondrously with you: and my people shall never be ashamed.

Joel 2:26

As believers, we must be careful not to limit God in our individual lives to what the world says is so.

Kenneth Copeland

And Jesus looking upon them saith, With men it is impossible, but not with God: for with God all things are possible.

Mark 10:27

23

The only way God's blessing will follow you is if you make up your mind to have no other gods before Him.

Norvel Hayes

No man can serve two masters: for either he will hate the one, and love the other; or else he will hold to the one, and despise the other. Ye cannot serve God and mammon.

Matthew 6:24

24

Our heavenly Father delights in giving His children good things, but only if we are not seeking after them.

Joyce Meyer

But seek (aim at and strive after) first of all His kingdom and His righteousness (His way of doing and being right), and then all these things taken together will be given you besides.

Matthew 6:33 AMP

Prosperity makes sense when it is motivated, not by selfishness, but by a sincere desire to bless others.

Dick Mills

Not rendering evil for evil, or railing for railing: but contrariwise blessing; knowing that ye are thereunto called, that ye should inherit a blessing.

1 Peter 3:9

26

Think of the joy your money will bring to the lives of those who will be saved or delivered through it.

John Avanzini

Heal the sick, cleanse the lepers, raise the dead, cast out devils: freely ye have received, freely give.

Matthew 10:8

27

You won't get out of debt overnight, but if you take it step-by-step and apply the principles of God's Word, you will reach your goal.

David Crank

That ye be not slothful, but followers of them who through faith and patience inherit the promises.

Hebrews 6:12

The Bible says plainly that God will cause us to have the hidden wealth of the world, the hidden riches of the secret places.

Kenneth Copeland

And I will give thee the treasures of darkness, and hidden riches of secret places, that thou mayest know that I, the LORD, which call thee by thy name, am the God of Israel.

Isaiah 45:3

29

If we take care
of God's house,
He will take care
of our house.

Kenneth Hagin, Jr.

*Those that be
planted in the house
of the LORD shall
flourish in the
courts of our God.
They shall still bring
forth fruit in old
age; they shall be
fat and flourishing.*

Psalm 92:13,14

God will not bless selfishness, and He will not bless laziness.

Norvel Hayes

He becometh poor that dealeth with a slack hand: but the hand of the diligent maketh rich.

Proverbs 10:4

31

Covenant people should live better than the world lives.

Jerry Savelle

And all nations shall call you blessed: for ye shall be a delightsome land, saith the LORD of hosts.

Malachi 3:12

32

It's not wrong to have money; it's wrong for money to have you.

Kenneth Hagin

For the love of money is the root of all evil: which while some coveted after, they have erred from the faith, and pierced themselves through with many sorrows.

1 Timothy 6:10

33

Wealth and poverty are just symptoms of a deeper root which is the attitude of the heart of man.

Rodney Howard-Browne

And be not conformed to this world: but be ye transformed by the renewing of your mind, that ye may prove what is that good, and acceptable, and perfect, will of God.

Romans 12:2

34

Many people get no blessing because they did not thank God for the last one.

Smith Wigglesworth

In every thing give thanks: for this is the will of God in Christ Jesus concerning you.

1 Thessalonians 5:18

The body of Christ is a military organization provided for by the King. He has made provision for all that we will ever need.

Kenneth Copeland

Who goeth a warfare any time at his own charges? who planteth a vineyard, and eateth not of the fruit thereof? or who feedeth a flock, and eateth not of the milk of the flock?

1 Corinthians 9:7

36

If it were sinful for you to enjoy material blessings, then God would not have created them nor promised that you may have them.

T. L. Osborn

Yea, the LORD shall give that which is good; and our land shall yield her increase.

Psalm 85:12

The sooner we take the attitude that we belong to Him and let Him rule over our finances, the sooner His provision will begin to flow our way.

Kenneth Copeland

And this they did, not as we hoped, but first gave their own selves to the Lord, and unto us by the will of God.

2 Corinthians 8:5

One of the rewards of faithful tithing is that God will open up the windows of heaven and pour out a blessing which is greater than you can contain.

David Crank

Bring ye all the tithes into the storehouse, that there may be meat in mine house, and prove me now herewith, saith the LORD of hosts, if I will not open you the windows of heaven, and pour you out a blessing, that there shall not be room enough to receive it.

Malachi 3:10

In any situation you face, you look to God as your Source, plant a seed out of your need, and expect a miracle to happen.

Richard Roberts

Now he who supplies seed to the sower and bread for food will also supply and increase your store of seed and will enlarge the harvest of your righteousness.

2 Corinthians 9:10

40

God can do some-thing great with your "nothing," but it takes obedience to clear the way for God to do a miracle.

R. W. Schambach

If ye be willing and obedient, ye shall eat the good of the land.

Isaiah 1:19

41

You can't give away your money by giving to the poor. You are actually lending to the Lord, and He will repay you.

Kenneth Copeland

He that hath pity upon the poor lendeth unto the LORD; and that which he hath given will he pay him again.

Proverbs 19:17

42

God's will is that we have so much treasure, we not only take care of our own needs, but help others too!

David Crank

Let him that stole steal no more: but rather let him labour, working with his hands the thing which is good, that he may have to give to him that needeth.

Ephesians 4:28

43

When you give, know that you are not subject to the whimsical fate of luck; instead, you are anchoring your future to God's superior principles of biblical economics.

John Avanzini

44

And by knowledge shall the chambers be filled with all precious and pleasant riches.

Proverbs 24:4

Begin to see yourself with God's best all around you and then you begin to speak that out of your mouth and you will have it in your life.

Casey Treat

For verily I say unto you, That whosoever shall say unto this mountain, Be thou removed, and be thou cast into the sea; and shall not doubt in his heart, but shall believe that those things which he saith shall come to pass; he shall have whatsoever he saith.

Mark 11:23

45

Your practice of praise power manifests the forces that will break every chain and bring abundance of blessing.

Don Gossett

O let the nations be glad and sing for joy: for thou shalt judge the people righteously, and govern the nations upon earth. Selah. Let the people praise thee, O God; let all the people praise thee.

Psalm 67:4,5

God's best is for His people to be totally free from all bondage . . . . including financial debt.

Jerry Savelle

The rich ruleth over the poor, and the borrower is servant to the lender.

Proverbs 22:7

47

God will bless us when we get involved with His plan and learn how to operate through tithes and offerings.

Fred Price

Will a man rob God? Yet ye have robbed me. But ye say, Wherein have we robbed thee? In tithes and offerings.

Malachi 3:8

48

You cannot invest thousands [of dollars] before investing just one . . . . start where you are with what you have.

Ed Cole

For if there be first a willing mind, it is accepted according to that a man hath, and not according to that he hath not.

2 Corinthians 8:12

49

Prosperity in abundance is the heritage of those who honor the Lord with their substance.

Bob Yandian

Honour the LORD with thy substance, and with the firstfruits of all thine increase: So shall thy barns be filled with plenty, and thy presses shall burst out with new wine.

Proverbs 3:9,10

If God made Abraham rich yesterday, He can make us rich today.

Fred Price

And Abram was very rich in cattle, in silver, and in gold.

Genesis 13:2

51

One of the reasons why Christians suffer poverty is lack of knowledge.

Ray McCauley

My people are destroyed for lack of knowledge: because thou hast rejected knowledge, I will also reject thee, that thou shalt be no priest to me: seeing thou hast forgotten the law of thy God, I will also forget thy children.

Hosea 4:6

52

God wants to reveal ways for you to profit and succeed financially.

Mike Murdock

Thus saith the LORD, thy Redeemer, the Holy One of Israel; I am the LORD thy God which teacheth thee to profit, which leadeth thee by the way that thou shouldest go.

Isaiah 48:17

53

Before you and I can
expect a harvest
of the miracles we
need in our lives,
we must plant a
seed of our faith.

Richard Roberts

*While the earth
remaineth, seedtime
and harvest . . . shall
not cease.*

Genesis 8:22

54

Many are waiting for their ship to come in who never sent one out.

Kenneth Copeland

Cast thy bread upon the waters: for thou shalt find it after many days.

Ecclesiastes 11:1

55

Unless you begin to develop a receiving mentality, God cannot begin to bring prosperity into your life.

John Avanzini

Now ye Philippians know also, that in the beginning of the gospel, when I departed from Macedonia, no church communicated with me as concerning giving and receiving, but ye only.

Philippians 4:15

56

If you are living in poverty and lack and want, change what you are saying. It will change what you have.

Kenneth Copeland

A man's belly shall be satisfied with the fruit of his mouth; and with the increase of his lips shall he be filled.

Proverbs 18:20

57

God expects us all
to be hard workers.
If you want to be rich,
be diligent.

Marilyn Hickey

He becometh poor
that dealeth with a
slack hand: but the
hand of the diligent
maketh rich.

Proverbs 10:4

58

When you help meet the needs of God's workers, He will meet your needs.

John Avanzini

Therefore all things whatsoever ye would that men should do to you, do ye even so to them: for this is the law and the prophets.

Matthew 7:12

59

The massive amounts of wealth on this earth were not meant for the sinner. They were meant for the children of God.

Anonymous

A good man leaveth an inheritance to his children's children: and the wealth of the sinner is laid up for the just.

Proverbs 13:22

60

God's financial plan is designed so that you can be a channel for the things of this world to be put into the Kingdom of God.

Fred Price

Distributing to the necessity of saints; given to hospitality.

Romans 12:13

61

The attitude with which you give is what God sees.

Rodney Howard-Browne

But the LORD said unto Samuel, Look not on his countenance, or on the height of his stature; because I have refused him: for the LORD seeth not as man seeth; for man looketh on the outward appearance, but the LORD looketh on the heart.

1 Samuel 16:7

62

Investing in the Kingdom of God is a sure thing.

Kenneth Copeland

And he sought God in the days of Zechariah, who had understanding in the visions of God: and as long as he sought the Lord, God made him to prosper.

2 Chronicles 26:5

63

God calls lack a curse and there is no way it could ever be a blessing.

Kenneth Copeland

So shall thy poverty come as one that travelleth, and thy want as an armed man.

Proverbs 6:11

64

You should refuse lack just as quickly as you refuse sickness.

Gloria Copeland

Submit yourselves therefore to God. Resist the devil, and he will flee from you.

James 4:7

65

You need faith to get rich. Because faith works by love, if you want to be wealthy, you need to start loving.

Marilyn Hickey

And they rose early in the morning, and went forth into the wilderness of Tekoa: and as they went forth, Jehoshaphat stood and said, Hear me, O Judah, and ye inhabitants of Jerusalem; Believe in the LORD your God, so shall ye be established; believe his prophets, so shall ye prosper.

2 Chronicles 20:20

You begin to walk in divine prosperity with a decision to no longer allow Satan to put symptoms of lack on you.

Gloria Copeland

And the seventy returned again with joy, saying, Lord, even the devils are subject unto us through thy name.

Luke 10:17

67

Unless you are willing to obey God and to submit to the Lordship of Jesus Christ, you may never receive very much in the way of prosperity or blessings at all.

Norvel Hayes

If they obey and serve him, they shall spend their days in prosperity, and their years in pleasures.

Job 36:11

68

God insists that we consecrate ourselves wholly unto Him. This is the only way we will enter into divine prosperity.

Jerry Savelle

But seek ye first the kingdom of God, and his righteousness; and all these things shall be added unto you.

Matthew 6:33

69

You can believe for divine prosperity just as you believe for divine health.

Gloria Copeland

Therefore I say unto you, What things soever ye desire, when ye pray, believe that ye receive them, and ye shall have them.

Mark 11:24

70

We have entered into the wealth of an inheritance from the God of the universe.

E. W. Kenyon

And of his fulness have all we received, and grace for grace.

John 1:16

God has always been a great giver!

John Avanzini

For by grace are ye saved through faith; and that not of yourselves: it is the gift of God.

Ephesians 2:8

72

God loves a cheerful giver.

Lester Sumrall

Every man according as he purposeth in his heart, so let him give; not grudgingly, or of necessity: for God loveth a cheerful giver.

2 Corinthians 9:7

73

Prosperity is standing under the shower on a Monday morning rejoicing, praising Jesus for the beautiful day and looking forward to going to work.

Ray McCauley

74

Wealth gotten by vanity shall be diminished: but he that gathereth by labour shall increase.

Proverbs 13:11

If you want to prosper according to biblical principles, you must forget most of the world's motives and principles of prosperity.

John Avanzini

But my God shall supply all your need according to his riches in glory by Christ Jesus.

Philippians 4:19

75

You cannot be God's Banker unless you are convinced that God wants you to prosper.

John Avanzini

The LORD did not set his love upon you, nor choose you, because ye were more in number than any people; for ye were the fewest of all people.

Deuteronomy 7:7

Heaven has nothing in it but victory and abundance, and God wants His kingdom to come to His earth.

Norvel Hayes

Thy kingdom come. Thy will be done in earth, as it is in heaven.

Matthew 6:10

Money is a great servant, but a terrible master.

Gloria Copeland

And he said unto them, Take heed, and beware of covetousness: for a man's life consisteth not in the abundance of the things which he possesseth.

Luke 12:15

78,

Jesus wants you rich – rich in Him as your Source.

Marilyn Hickey

Let them shout for joy, and be glad, that favour my righteous cause: yea, let them say continually, Let the LORD be magnified, which hath pleasure in the prosperity of his servant.

Psalm 35:27

79

May we always remember that God cannot bless and prosper any one or any ministry where there is bitterness, strife, and unforgiveness.

Paul F. Crouch, Sr.

And when ye stand praying, forgive, if ye have ought against any: that your Father also which is in heaven may forgive you your trespasses.

Mark 11:25

If you know how to believe God financially, start helping the people around you. You will begin to grow as you reach out to others.

Kenneth Copeland

Bear ye one another's burdens, and so fulfil the law of Christ.

Galatians 6:2

81

If you want something coming in on every wave, you must give on every wave.

Kenneth Hagin, Jr.

Cast thy bread upon the waters: for thou shalt find it after many days.

Ecclesiastes 11:1

Jesus Christ has an anti-poverty program, the poor.

John G. Lake

He who gives to the poor will not want, but he who hides his eyes [from their want] will have many a curse.

Proverbs 28:27 AMP

83

Jesus taught the law of expectation that could unlock the 100-fold return.

Mike Murdock

But he shall receive an hundredfold now in this time, houses, and brethren, and sisters, and mothers, and children, and lands, with persecutions; and in the world to come eternal life.

Mark 10:30

84

Poverty and prosperity are in the power of the tongue.

Casey Treat

Death and life are in the power of the tongue: and they that love it shall eat the fruit thereof.

Proverbs 18:21

85

One reason God wants you out of debt is so you are not pressed down by the weight of financial pressures.

David Crank

Be careful for nothing; but in every thing by prayer and supplication with thanksgiving let your requests be made known unto God.

Philippians 4:6

We have to burst the balloon of tradition that has left Christians with the attitude that it is a lack of spirituality to have possessions of any kind.

Fred Price

And also that nation, whom they shall serve, will I judge: and afterward shall they come out with great substance.

Genesis 15:14

It's not the amount given that is the greatest importance to God, but the percentage.

Charles Capps

Bring ye all the tithes into the storehouse, that there may be meat in mine house, and prove me now herewith, saith the LORD of hosts, if I will not open you the windows of heaven, and pour you out a blessing, that there shall not be room enough to receive it.

Malachi 3:10

88

If you have not received anything, it is because you have not given anything.

Fred Price

He that hath a bountiful eye shall be blessed; for he giveth of his bread to the poor.

Proverbs 22:9

89

The Word never tells us to sit back and wait for wealth. God empowers us to obtain wealth.

Marilyn Hickey

But thou shalt remember the LORD thy God: for it is he that giveth thee power to get wealth, that he may establish his covenant which he sware unto thy fathers, as it is this day.

Deuteronomy 8:18

Understand, you cannot be a blessing until you yourself are blessed.

Fred Price

And I will make of thee a great nation, and I will bless thee, and make thy name great; and thou shalt be a blessing.

Genesis 12:2

91

God is not moved by need; God is moved by faith.

John Avanzini

For the eyes of the LORD run to and fro throughout the whole earth, to show himself strong in the behalf of them whose heart is perfect toward him. Herein thou hast done foolishly: therefore from henceforth thou shalt have wars.

2 Chronicles 16:9

92

Worship God, and He will pay the bills.

Norvel Hayes

Let the people praise thee, O God; let all the people praise thee. Then shall the earth yield her increase; and God, even our own God, shall bless us.

Psalm 67:5,6

93

You must become seed-conscious, not need-conscious.

Jerry Savelle

And this they did, not as we hoped, but first gave their own selves to the LORD, and unto us by the will of God.

2 Corinthians 8:5

If you want a
bountiful crop,
you've got to
sow bountifully.

Kenneth Hagin

But this I say, He which soweth sparingly shall reap also sparingly; and he which soweth bountifully shall reap also bountifully.

2 Corinthians 9:6

95

God is not limited
to your income,
or farm, or salary,
or business, or stocks,
or securities,
or pensions,
or interest.

T. L. Osborn

O LORD, how manifold are thy works! in wisdom hast thou made them all: the earth is full of thy riches.

Psalm 104:24

The Father has a plan whereby you can become financially and materially independent of the circumstances.

Fred Price

"For I know the plans I have for you," declares the LORD, "plans to prosper you and not to harm you, plans to give you hope and a future."

Jeremiah 29:11 NIV

97

Plant your precious seeds in fertile ground and watch God unfold a financial miracle in your life.

John Avanzini

They that sow in tears shall reap in joy.

Psalm 126:5

If your motive is to be prosperous without serving God, you had better read some other book.

Gloria Copeland

But thou shalt remember the LORD thy God: for it is he that giveth thee power to get wealth, that he may establish his covenant which he sware unto thy fathers, as it is this day.

Deuteronomy 8:18

99

God's financial program will bring you the material things, but it will bring you much more if you will first seek the Lord.

Casey Treat

But seek ye first the kingdom of God, and his righteousness; and all these things shall be added unto you.

Matthew 6:33

God will never disappoint you, and you will never go wrong by doing what God asks you to do.

John Osteen

If you are willing and obedient, you will eat the best from the land.

Isaiah 1:19 NIV

101

You are to set your mind on things above and refuse to allow money or possessions to control your thinking and actions.

Gloria Copeland

102

Set your affection on things above, not on things on the earth.

Colossians 3:2

The measure you
use in giving
will determine the
measure that will be
applied to you in
receiving.

John Avanzini

*Give, and it shall be
given unto you;
good measure,
pressed down, and
shaken together, and
running over, shall
men give into your
bosom. For with the
same measure that
ye mete withal it
shall be measured to
you again.*

Luke 6:38

103

Speak the Word, not the circumstances, and you will get involved with God's financial program.

Casey Treat

For we walk by faith, not by sight.

2 Corinthians 5:7

104

Command the money you need to come to you; the authority is yours.

Gloria Copeland

Behold, I give unto you power to tread on serpents and scorpions, and over all the power of the enemy: and nothing shall by any means hurt you.

Luke 10:19

105

God would not give you the power to get wealth if He did not intend for you to use that power and become wealthy.

John Avanzini

But thou shalt remember the LORD thy God: for it is he that giveth thee power to get wealth, that he may establish his covenant which he sware unto thy fathers, as it is this day.

Deuteronomy 8:18

106

It is the responsibility of every member of the body of Christ to believe God for the abundance He provides.

Kenneth Copeland

For we walk by faith, not by sight.

2 Corinthians 5:7

107

No matter how far from God's plan of abundance you are now, when you begin to comply with God's spiritual laws of prosperity, He will overtake you with His blessings.

John Avanzini

The LORD shall command the blessing upon thee in thy storehouses, and in all that thou settest thine hand unto; and he shall bless thee in the land which the LORD thy God giveth thee.

Deuteronomy 28:8

What God has in mind is a financial, economic program to so bless you that all of your needs and desires which are consistent with a godly life will be met.

Fred Price

Fear not, little flock; for it is your Father's good pleasure to give you the kingdom.

Luke 12:32

109

Poverty is a curse and the Bible says that we have been redeemed from it.

Kenneth Copeland

Christ hath redeemed us from the curse of the law, being made a curse for us: for it is written, Cursed is every one that hangeth on a tree.

Galatians 3:13

Poverty came with sin. Adam and Eve never lacked anything before they sinned.

Ray McCauley

And God blessed them, and God said unto them, Be fruitful, and multiply, and replenish the earth, and subdue it: and have dominion over the fish of the sea, and over the fowl of the air, and over every living thing that moveth upon the earth.

Genesis 1:28

Never count pennies looking at omnipotence. Allow Christ to empty your hands, and He will fill them.

Jesse Duplantis

Now he that ministereth seed to the sower both minister bread for your food, and multiply your seed sown, and increase the fruits of your righteousness.

2 Corinthians 9:10

When you are faithful with the things God already has given you, then He will give you something better.

Norvel Hayes

His lord said unto him, Well done, thou good and faithful servant: thou hast been faithful over a few things, I will make thee ruler over many things: enter thou into the joy of thy lord.

Matthew 25:21

Life is intended to be of such quality that we enjoy it immensely.

Joyce Meyer

The thief comes only in order to steal and kill and destroy. I came that they may have and enjoy life, and have it in abundance (to the full, till it overflows.)

John 10:10 AMP

Tell the ministering angels to go forth and bring you what is needed.

Kenneth Hagin

Are they not all ministering spirits, sent forth to minister for them who shall be heirs of salvation?

Hebrews 1:14

115

We need to learn how to make the proper deposits in our heavenly bank so that we can withdraw from it when needed.

Kenneth Copeland

Not because I desire a gift: but I desire fruit that may abound to your account.

Philippians 4:17

116

God created all the wealth of this earth — not for believers to monopolize, but for the prosperity of His children who do His will.

T. L. Osborn

And ye shall eat in plenty, and be satisfied, and praise the name of the LORD your God, that hath dealt wondrously with you: and my people shall never be ashamed.

Joel 2:26

117

You ask for the finances for that undertaking for the Lord: your business is to ask; His business is to see that it is done.

E. W. Kenyon

And if we know that he hear us, whatsoever we ask, we know that we have the petitions that we desired of him.

1 John 5:15

118

Godly prosperity and health begin on the inside of your soul.

Billy Joe Daugherty

Beloved, I wish above all things that thou mayest prosper and be in health, even as thy soul prospereth.

3 John 1:2

119

The wisdom of God will show you how to get rich.

Marilyn Hickey

Doth not wisdom cry? and understanding put forth her voice? Riches and honour are with me; yea, durable riches and righteousness.

Proverbs 8:1,18

120

Hard workers will have plenty of bread.

John Avanzini

He that tilleth his land shall have plenty of bread: but he that followeth after vain persons shall have poverty enough.

Proverbs 28:19

Prosperity requires effort.

Bob Yandian

Wealth gotten by vanity shall be diminished: but he that gathereth by labour shall increase.

Proverbs 13:11

122

The Bible promises you a place financially where you will be satisfied.

Rod Parsley

A man shall be satisfied with good by the fruit of his mouth: and the recompense of a man's hands shall be rendered unto him.

Proverbs 12:14

Your future financial condition will be determined by your obedience today.

John Avanzini

Be not deceived; God is not mocked: for whatsoever a man soweth, that shall he also reap.

Galatians 6:7

124

Every good thing is for us on the holy line, walking uprightly, being set free, being made God's property.

Smith Wigglesworth

For the LORD God is a sun and shield: the LORD will give grace and glory: no good thing will he withhold from them that walk uprightly.

Psalm 84:11

Prosperity and success are the inevitable by-products of being a mediator-doer of God's Word.

Creflo Dollar, Jr.

Do not let this Book of the Law depart from your mouth; meditate on it day and night, so that you may be careful to do everything written in it. Then you will be prosperous and successful.

Joshua 1:8 NIV

126

You can't beat God givin', no matter how you try . . . .

R. W. Schambach

Now unto him that is able to do exceeding abundantly above all that we ask or think, according to the power that worketh in us . . . .

Ephesians 3:20

He [God] is not limited to what we have or who we are.

Kathryn Kuhlman

The earth is the LORD'S, and the fulness thereof; the world, and they that dwell therein.

Psalm 24:1

128

God uses people who are faithful in their finances, and tithing is part of that faithfulness.

John Avanzini

His lord said unto him, Well done, thou good and faithful servant: thou hast been faithful over a few things, I will make thee ruler over many things: enter thou into the joy of thy lord.

Matthew 25:21

Don't eat your seed!

Charles Capps

But this I say, He which soweth sparingly shall reap also sparingly; and he which soweth bountifully shall reap also bountifully.

2 Corinthians 9:6

130

When we trust God even in our need, He knows how to open doors we never dreamed possible.

R. W. Schambach

And being fully persuaded that, what he had promised, he was able also to perform.

Romans 4:21

When God talks to your finances, Satan cannot stop it from coming to pass.

Jerry Savelle

The LORD shall command the blessing upon thee in thy storehouses, and in all that thou settest thine hand unto; and he shall bless thee in the land which the LORD thy God giveth thee.

Deuteronomy 28:8

132

Our Father,
El Shaddai, is more
than enough to meet
every need, in every
crisis, at any time.

Anonymous

*And will be a Father
unto you, and ye
shall be my sons
and daughters, saith
the LORD Almighty.*

2 Corinthians 6:18

133

Jesus took the time to show His disciples where to get money to pay their taxes.

Mike Murdock

Notwithstanding, lest we should offend them, go thou to the sea, and cast an hook, and take up the fish that first cometh up; and when thou hast opened his mouth, thou shalt find a piece of money: that take, and give unto them for me and thee.

Matthew 17:27

134

Prosperity means the ability to meet any given need at any given time through the power of God.

Ray McCauley

The eyes of your understanding being enlightened; that ye may know what is the hope of his calling, and what the riches of the glory of his inheritance in the saints, And what is the exceeding greatness of his power to us-ward who believe, according to the working of his mighty power.

Ephesians 1:18,19

135

Prosperity enables you to be about your Father's business.

Kenneth Copeland

As it is written, He hath dispersed abroad; he hath given to the poor: his righteousness remaineth for ever.

2 Corinthians 9:9

If it is God's will to prosper you, anything less is out of God's will.

Rod Parsley

In the house of the righteous is much treasure: but in the revenues of the wicked is trouble.

Proverbs 15:6

137

If you have nothing, you can do nothing.

Ray McCauley

Let him that stole steal no more: but rather let him labour, working with his hands the thing which is good, that he may have to give to him that needeth.

Ephesians 4:28

138

It is godly to give expecting to receive.

John Avanzini

Give, and it shall be given unto you; good measure, pressed down, and shaken together, and running over, shall men give into your bosom. For with the same measure that ye mete withal it shall be measured to you again.

Luke 6:38

139

God's pleasure increases when His servants prosper.

Mack and Brenda Timberlake

Let them shout for joy, and be glad, that favour my righteous cause: yea, let them say continually, Let the LORD be magnified, which hath pleasure in the prosperity of his servant.

Psalm 35:27

140

You will never get out of debt until you come to the point where you really believe that it can happen to you, too.

David Crank

Jesus said unto him, If thou canst believe, all things are possible to him that believeth.

Mark 9:23

141

Sow generously during the famine.

John Avanzini

Then Isaac sowed in that land, and received in the same year an hundredfold: and the LORD blessed him.

Genesis 26:12

All that we possess
is provided for us
by God, and He
asks that we return
a portion of it to Him.

Lester Sumrall

*And all the tithe of
the land, whether of
the seed of the land,
or of the fruit of the
tree, is the LORD'S:
it is holy unto the
LORD.*

Leviticus 27:30

143

If you let go of what's in your hand toward God, then God will let go of what is in His hand toward you.

Oral Roberts

A generous man will prosper; he who refreshes others will himself be refreshed.

Proverbs 11:25 NIV

144

It is not just a matter
of whether God is
pouring out blessings;
it is a matter of
whether you are
in a position to
receive them.

Buddy Harrison

Therefore I say unto you, What things soever ye desire, when ye pray, believe that ye receive them, and ye shall have them.

Mark 11:24

145

The reason God
is unable to bless
His people with
abundance is because
most have their hands
gripped on their own
meager substance.

Jesse Duplantis

146

*He that giveth unto
the poor shall not
lack: but he that
hideth his eyes shall
have many a curse.*

Proverbs 28:27

One of the best reasons for being out of debt is that you'll be able to give more into the kingdom to preach the gospel.

David Crank

But thou shalt remember the LORD thy God: for it is he that giveth thee power to get wealth, that he may establish his covenant which he sware unto thy fathers, as it is this day.

Deuteronomy 8:18

If all you're doing is trying to get by 'til payday, how can you help anyone else?

Casey Treat

Let him that stole steal no more: but rather let him labour, working with his hands the thing which is good, that he may have to give to him that needeth.

Ephesians 4:28

148

The more faithful you are to use and give your money to God and His work, the more He showers His blessings upon you.

Norvel Hayes

His lord said unto him, Well done, thou good and faithful servant: thou hast been faithful over a few things, I will make thee ruler over many things: enter thou into the joy of thy lord.

Matthew 25:21

149

What we have is not ours, we are merely stewards of all that belongs to God.

Gloria Copeland

Moreover it is required in stewards, that a man be found faithful.

1 Corinthians 4:2

150

If you will esteem Jesus as your wealth, He will pour blessings and riches on you.

Marilyn Hickey

For ye know the grace of our LORD Jesus Christ, that, though he was rich, yet for your sakes he became poor, that ye through his poverty might be rich.

2 Corinthians 8:9

151

God did not promise we would have a lean supply, but a rich supply. We're abundantly provided for!

Kenneth Hagin

152

And God is able to make all grace abound toward you; that ye, always having all sufficiency in all things, may abound to every good work.

2 Corinthians 9:8

All wealth is His
creation, and He has
unlimited ways to
place it into your
hands for His glory.

T. L. Osborn

*The earth is the
LORD'S, and the
fulness thereof;
the world, and they
that dwell therein.*

Psalm 24:1

153

True prosperity is the ability to use God's power to meet the needs of mankind in any realm of life.

Kenneth Copeland

This book of the law shall not depart out of thy mouth; but thou shalt meditate therein day and night, that thou mayest observe to do according to all that is written therein: for then thou shalt make thy way prosperous, and then thou shalt have good success.

Joshua 1:8

154

Think of the highest, the richest, the best and the most. God is able to do above it all.

Billy Joe Daugherty

Now unto him that is able to do exceeding abundantly above all that we ask or think, according to the power that worketh in us.

Ephesians 3:20

155

PRAYER FOR PROSPERITY

Father, in the name of Your Son, Jesus, I confess Your Word over my finances this day. As I do this, I say it with my mouth and believe it in my heart and know that Your Word will not return to You void, but will accomplish what it says it will do.

Therefore, I believe in the name of Jesus that all my needs are met, according to Philippians 4:19. I believe that because I have given tithes and offerings to further your cause, Father, gifts will be given to me, good measure, pressed down, shaken together, and running over will they pour into my bosom. For with the measure I deal out, it will be measured back to me.

Father, You have delivered me out of the authority of darkness into the Kingdom of Your dear Son. Father, I have taken my place as your child. I thank You that You have assumed Your place as my Father and have made Your home with me. You are taking care of me and even now are enabling me to walk in love and in wisdom, and to walk in the fullness of fellowship with Your Son.

Satan, I bind you from my finances, according to Matthew 18:18, and loose you from your assignment against me, in the name of Jesus.

Scripture References

Ephesians 1:3	Psalm 112:3	Acts 16:31	Colossians 3:14,15
Proverbs 24:3,4	Luke 6:48	Philippians 2:10,11	Acts 20:32
Proverbs 15:6	Acts 4:11	Colossians 3:23	Joshua 24:15
Proverbs 12:7			

Father, I thank You that Your ministering spirits are now free to minister for me and bring in the necessary finances.

Father, I confess You are a very present help in trouble, and You are more than enough. I confess, God, You are able to make all grace — every favor and earthly blessing — come to me in abundance, so that I am always, and in all circumstances furnished in abundance for every good work and charitable donation.

Scripture References

Isaiah 55:11	2 Corinthians 6:16,18
Philippians 4:19	Matthew 18:18
Luke 6:38	Hebrews 1:14
Mark 10:29,30	2 Corinthians 9:8
Colossians 1:13	Psalm 46:1

DEDICATION FOR YOUR TITHES

I profess this day unto the Lord God that I have come into the inheritance which the Lord swore to give me. I am in the land which You have provided for me in Jesus Christ, the Kingdom of Almighty God. I was a sinner serving Satan; he was my god. But I called upon the name of Jesus, and You heard my cry and delivered me into the Kingdom of Your dear Son.

Jesus, as my Lord and High Priest, I bring the first fruits of my income to You and worship the Lord my God with it.

I rejoice in all the good which You have given to me and my household. I have hearkened to the voice of the Lord my God and have done according to all that He has commanded me. Now look down from Your holy habitation from heaven and bless me as You said in Your Word. I thank You, Father, in Jesus' name.

Scripture References

Deuteronomy 26:1,3,10,11,14,15
Ephesians 2:1-5

Colossians 1:13
Hebrews 3:1,7,8

Additional copies of this book and
Faith's Little Instruction Book I and *II* and
Faith's Little Instruction for Healing
are available from your local bookstore.

P. O. Box 35035
Tulsa, Oklahoma 74153

In Canada contact:

Word Alive
P. O. Box 284
Niverville, Manitoba
CANADA ROA 1EO

The Harrison House Vision

Proclaiming the truth and the power
Of the Gospel of Jesus Christ
With excellence;

Challenging Christians to
Live victoriously,
Grow spiritually,
Know God intimately.